THE LITTLE BOOK OF

THE 1960s

MIX
Paper | Supporting
responsible forestry
FSC® C144853

Published in 2024 by OH!
An Imprint of Welbeck Non-Fiction Limited,
part of Welbeck Publishing Group.
Offices in: London – 20 Mortimer Street, London W1T 3JW
and Sydney – Level 17, 207 Kent St, Sydney NSW 2000 Australia
www.welbeckpublishing.com

Compilation text © Welbeck Non-Fiction Limited 2023
Design © Welbeck Non-Fiction Limited 2023

ISBN 978-1-80069-569-6

Compiled and written by: Stella Caldwell
Editorial: Matt Tomlinson
Project manager: Russell Porter
Production: Arlene Lestrade

A CIP catalogue record for this book is available from the British Library

Printed in China

10 9 8 7 6 5 4 3 2 1

THE LITTLE BOOK OF

the nineteen

60s

peace, love and revolution

OH!

CONTENTS

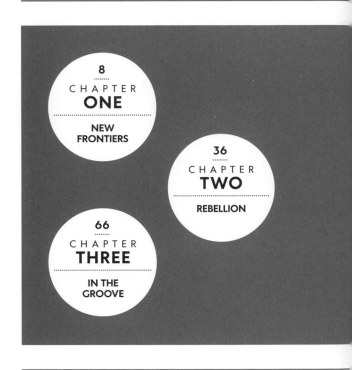

INTRODUCTION

At the heart of the 1960s was a desire for change, a yearning for a new way of living and a rejection of the old order. Politically dominated by the Cold War and the Cuban Missile Crisis, the decade was also an era of protest. Civil rights activists called for an end to racism, anti-war protestors railed against the Vietnam War, women's rights campaigners advocated for gender equality and the burgeoning LGBTQ+ movement dared to dream of a world free of discrimination.

The counterculture blossomed, captivating hearts and minds with its bold rejection of conventional norms, while hippies called for peace, love and social justice. Amidst the turbulence, the arts emerged as a powerful force for expression. Visionary artists like Warhol and Lichtenstein pushed boundaries, while literature and popular music resonated with the desire for change.

Fashion reflected the spirit of rebellion and individuality that defined the era. The boundary-pushing styles of miniskirts, bell-bottoms and psychedelic prints embodied the quest for self-expression and the rejection of conformity.

The decade also witnessed remarkable advancements in innovation, science and sport. The Space Race fuelled an extraordinary leap forward as Neil Armstrong and Buzz Aldrin became the first humans to walk on the moon. Boxer Muhammad Ali became a sporting icon, technological breakthroughs and medical discoveries promised a brighter future, while wacky toys and the first digital video game, Spacewar!, captured the imaginations of a new generation of children.

Packed full of fabulous facts and quirky asides, *The Little Book of the 1960s* will take you on an evocative journey through the twists and turns of this revolutionary era. With inspiring quotes from key figures such as Martin Luther King Jr, Harper Lee and The Beatles, it's the perfect guide to the events, icons and ideas that defined the '60s.

the nineteen 60s

Chapter **1**
new frontiers

In the 1960s, global politics was a complex landscape of ideological clashes and geopolitical tensions. The Cold War dominated international relations, while the shocking assassination of President John F. Kennedy in 1963 had profound implications for the world.

Meanwhile, echoes of Czechoslovakia's 1968 "Prague Spring" reverberated globally, sparking protests and debates about the Cold War and communism.

66

We stand today on the edge
of a new frontier – the frontier
of the 1960s, a frontier of
unknown opportunities and
perils, a frontier of unfulfilled
hopes and threats...

99

John F. Kennedy
Acceptance speech for the presidential nomination
at the National Democratic Convention, 15 July 1960

"

Ask not what your country
can do for you – ask what
you can do for your country.

"

John F. Kennedy
Inaugural Address, 20 January 1961

"

He who rejects change is the architect of decay. The only human institution which rejects progress is the cemetery.

"

Harold Wilson
The British prime minister in 1964, in a speech to the Consultive Assembly of the Council of Europe, 23 January 1967

"

Being president is like being
a jackass in a hailstorm. There's
nothing to do but to stand
there and take it.

"

Lyndon B. Johnson
US president from 1963 until 1969, in advice
given to his successor, Robert Nixon, 1969

The Bay of Pigs

On 17 April 1961, the US launched a full-scale invasion of Cuba to topple its leader, Fidel Castro. CIA-trained Cuban exiles landed at beaches along the Bay of Pigs, but the poorly planned operation led to a swift defeat for the invading forces.

The failure not only embarrassed the US but also solidified Castro's grip on power – and further strained relations between Cuba and the US.

"

The worse I do, the more popular I get.

"

John F. Kennedy

The US president on his high approval rating in the
wake of the Bay of Pigs fiasco, 1962

Cold War Division

On 13 August 1961, the construction of the Berlin Wall began, dividing East and West Berlin. Erected by the German Democratic Republic (GDR) to halt the mass exodus of East Germans to the West, the structure spanned 96 miles (155km).

With families separated, the wall became a powerful symbol of the Cold War division. It would stand for almost 28 years, until its fall in 1989.

" I take pride in the words *Ich bin ein Berliner.*

John F. Kennedy
West Berlin, 26 June 1963.
The German words mean "I am a Berliner".

Cuban Missile Crisis

In October 1962, the world was seemingly brought to the brink of nuclear war with the US discovery that the Soviet Union was placing nuclear missiles in Cuba. President John F. Kennedy imposed a naval blockade around Cuba and after days of intense negotiations, the Soviets agreed to dismantle the weapon sites.

In a separate deal – which remained secret for more than 25 years – the US also agreed to remove its nuclear missiles from Turkey.

"

We're eyeball to eyeball, and I think the other fellow just blinked.

"

Dean Rusk
The US Secretary of State, after Soviet ships
approached to within just a few miles of a US naval
blockade before turning back, October 1962

Death of JFK

On 22 November 1963, the 35th president of the US, John F. Kennedy, was shot and fatally wounded while riding in a motorcade in Dallas, Texas. The assassination of the popular young president sent shockwaves around the world.

Lee Harvey Oswald was arrested as the primary suspect but was himself killed before standing trial – dying at the same hospital as Kennedy, two days after the president.

"

The real 1960s began on the afternoon of November 22, 1963. It came to seem that Kennedy's murder opened some malign trap door in American culture, and the wild bats flapped out.

"

Lance Morrow
American writer and essayist

Nelson Mandela

In 1964, Nelson Mandela was imprisoned on Robben Island for his opposition to South Africa's strict apartheid laws.

Enduring 27 years in captivity, his incarceration would become a symbol of the country's struggle against racial segregation while his resilience and leadership made him a global icon for justice and equality.

"

It is said that no one truly knows a nation until one has been inside its jails. A nation should not be judged by how it treats its highest citizens, but its lowest ones.

"

Nelson Mandela

Iron Lady

In 1966, Indira Gandhi – nicknamed the "Iron Lady of India" – became the first female prime minister of India. Serving in the role until 1977 – and again from 1980 until her assassination in 1984 – she played a crucial role in shaping India's political landscape.

Known for her strong leadership, she implemented social and economic reforms, pursued a policy of non-alignment and promoted the empowerment of women.

"

I am in no sense a feminist, but I believe in women being able to do everything... Given the opportunity to develop, capable Indian women have come to the top at once.

"

Indira Gandhi

India's first female prime minister

A New Flag

Prior to 1965, Canada used the Red Ensign flag, which featured the Union Jack in the canton. However, after much debate and controversy, the current maple leaf flag was officially introduced on 15 February 1965.

Designed by George F. G. Stanley and inspired by the national emblem of Canada, the new flag symbolized Canadian identity, unity and independence.

Six-Day War

In June 1967, war broke out between Israel and its neighbouring Arab states. After launching a pre-emptive strike against Egypt, Jordan and Syria, Israel captured the Sinai Peninsula, Gaza Strip, West Bank and East Jerusalem, declaring victory after just six days.

The war reshaped the Middle East, leading to significant territorial changes, increased tensions and lasting consequences for Israeli-Arab relations.

Mystery at Sea

Australia's 17th prime minister, Harold Holt, disappeared on 17 December 1967, while swimming at Cheviot Beach near Melbourne.

Despite extensive search efforts, his body was never found and he was presumed dead. His disappearance remains a mystery and has given rise to various conspiracy theories and speculation.

66

Look Tony, what are the odds of a prime minister being drowned or taken by a shark?

99

Harold Holt

Part of a private conversation with his press secretary, Tony Eggleton, shortly before his disappearance while swimming in December 1967

The Prague Spring

Since the end of the Second World War, Czechoslovakia had been a communist country, controlled by Moscow. But in January 1968, under the leadership of Alexander Dubček, the country aimed for "socialism with a human face", calling for political reforms, freedom of speech and reduced censorship.

The so-called "Prague Spring" caused alarm among Soviet leaders, leading to the eventual invasion in August 1968 to suppress the movement.

"

They may crush the flowers, but they cannot stop the Spring.

"

Alexander Dubček

His response to the Soviet invasion of Czechoslovakia
to crush the Prague Spring, August 1968

Civil War in Nigeria

In July 1967, the Biafran War broke out, resulting in a tragic loss of life. The conflict erupted when the southeastern region of Nigeria declared independence as the Republic of Biafra.

The war witnessed brutal battles, famine and humanitarian crises, leaving a lasting impact on the nation's political landscape for years to come.

The Troubles Begin

The Northern Ireland Troubles, a period of intense sectarian conflict and political violence, began in the late 1960s. Characterized by clashes between nationalist and unionist communities, paramilitary groups and security forces, the conflict emerged from deep-rooted divisions over British rule and Irish nationalism, as well as social and economic inequalities.

NPT

The Nuclear Non-Proliferation Treaty (NPT), aimed at preventing the spread of nuclear weapons, was opened for signature in 1968.

The NPT has three pillars: non-proliferation, disarmament and peaceful use of nuclear energy.

66

Today, every inhabitant of this planet must contemplate the day when this planet may no longer be habitable. Every man, woman and child lives under a nuclear sword of Damocles, hanging by the slenderest of threads, capable of being cut at any moment by accident or miscalculation or by madness. The weapons of war must be abolished before they abolish us.

99

John F. Kennedy
Address before the General Assembly
of the United Nations, 25 September 1961

the nineteen 60s

Chapter 2
rebellion

"The Times They Are a-Changin'" crooned Bob Dylan in 1964. Fuelled by anti-war sentiments, civil rights activism and a desire for personal freedom, the counterculture of the 1960s kicked back against mainstream values and norms and called for peace, individualism and mind-bending experimentation.

Music, art and literature all expressed countercultural ideals, with musicians and writers becoming iconic symbols of the movement.

66

The thing the sixties did was
to show us the possibilities
and the responsibility that we all
had. It wasn't the answer.
It just gave us a glimpse of
the possibility.

99

John Lennon

"

This is the story of America.
Everybody's doing what they
think they're supposed to do.

"

Jack Kerouac
On the Road, 1957. Although it was written
towards the end of the 1950s, this cult classic heavily
influenced the counterculture of the 1960s.

Fight for Free Speech

In 1964, the Free Speech Movement emerged on the campus of the University of California, Berkeley. Students demanded the right to advocate for political causes on campus and challenged the university's restrictions. Their activism sparked nationwide debates about civil liberties, student rights and the power of dissent.

""

There is a time when the operation of the machine becomes so odious, makes you so sick at heart, that you can't take part! You can't even passively take part! And you've got to put your bodies upon the gears and upon the wheels... upon the levers, upon all the apparatus, and you've got to make it stop!

""

Mario Savio

A key member of the Berkeley Free Speech Movement, from his famous "Bodies Upon the Gears" address, 2 December 1964

"

Turn on, tune in, drop out.

"

Timothy Leary

From a speech he gave at the Human Be-In
gathering in San Francisco, 14 January 1967

Timothy Leary claimed his famous phrase, "Turn on, tune in, drop out" came to him while taking a shower. He had been asked to come up with "something snappy" to promote the benefits of using psychedelic substances, such as LSD.

Usually when you ask somebody in college why they are there, they'll tell you it's to get an education. The truth of it is, they are there to get the degree so that they can get ahead in the rat race. Too many college radicals are two-timing punks. The only reason you should be in college is to destroy it.

Abbie Hoffman

Steal This Book, 1971. Written by one of the most influential activists of the late 1960s, this bestselling book exemplified the counterculture of the 1960s.

66

Bob Dylan was different. Where most folk singers were either clean-cut or homey looking, Dylan had wild long hair. He resembled a poor white dropout of questionable morals. His songs were hard-driving, powerful, intense. It was hard to be neutral about them. "The Times They Are a-Changing" was perhaps the first song to exploit the generation gap.

99

William L. O'Neill

Coming Apart – An Informal History of America in the 1960s, 1974

66

When I was young in the 1960s,
all the world watched the youth.
Everywhere was the sensation
of wanting to break the chains
but to do something beautiful.
It is my privilege to have beauty
always near me.

99

Yves Saint Laurent

66

It was a wonderful time to be young. The 1960s didn't end until about 1976. We all believed in Make Love, Not War. We were idealistic innocents, despite the drugs and sex.

99

Margot Kidder
American-Canadian actress

The Hippie Movement

Embracing peace, love and communal living, hippies – or "love children" – rejected mainstream values. Seeking alternative lifestyles, they wore colourful clothes, experimented with drugs and explored spirituality.

"

Dropouts on a Mission

"

Headline from a four-page special on the growth of
Hippie culture, *Newsweek*, 6 February 1967

Revolutionary Hero

A major figure of the Cuban Revolution, Che Guevara emerged as an iconic symbol of rebellion in the 1960s.

As a Marxist, his image and revolutionary ideals resonated with those seeking social change worldwide.

"

The revolution is not an apple that falls when it is ripe. You have to make it fall.

"

Che Guevara

Interview with *Libération*, March 1965

The Beats

The Beat Generation had a huge influence on the counterculture movements of the 1960s. The writings and ideas of authors such as Jack Kerouac, Allen Ginsberg and William S. Burroughs – who rebelled against the conventions of mainstream culture and stood for individualism and freedom of expression – chimed with the youth of the 1960s.

66

Follow your inner moonlight;
don't hide the madness. You say
what you want to say when you
don't care who's listening.

99

Allen Ginsberg
Key member of the Beat Generation

Woodstock Festival

This legendary festival, held in August 1969 in Bethel, New York, was a pivotal moment in music and counterculture history.

Over 400,000 people gathered for the event, featuring iconic performances from artists such as Jimi Hendrix, Janis Joplin and The Who.

"

I'm a farmer. I don't know how to speak to 20 people at one time, let alone a crowd like this. But I think you people have proven something to the world. This is the largest group of people ever assembled in one place. We had no idea that there would be this size group!

"

Max Yasgur
The dairy farmer who allowed his land to be used for the Woodstock festival, in his address to the crowd, 13 August 1969

___

"

The hippies wanted peace
and love. We wanted Ferraris,
blondes and switchblades.

"

Alice Cooper

___

"

Stranger: [giving Captain America some LSD]: "When you get to the right place, with the right people, quarter this. You know, this could be the right place. The time's running out."

Captain America: "Yeah, I'm, I'm hip about time. But I just gotta go.

"

From the iconic counterculture film *Easy Rider*, 1969

"

Yippies, Hippies, Yahoos, Black Panthers, lions and tigers alike – I would swap the whole damn zoo for the kind of young Americans I saw in Vietnam.

"

Spiro T. Agnew
Vice President of the United States under President Richard Nixon, during a speech delivered in Des Moines, Iowa, 13 November 1969

❝

In virtually every Western society in the 1960s there was a moral revolution, an abandonment of its entire traditional ethic of self-restraint.

❞

Jonathan Sacks
English Orthodox rabbi

The Acid Test

In the mid 1960s, author Ken Kesey – best known for his novel *One Flew Over the Cuckoo's Nest* – organized a series of parties called "Acid Tests". Intended to promote a message of expanded consciousness and personal freedom, guests were invited to experiment with the psychedelic drug LSD. The name was later popularized in Tom Wolfe's book *The Electric Kool-Aid Acid Test*.

" Can you pass the acid test? "

Slogan from a poster advertising one of
Ken Kesey's public "acid test" parties in the mid-1960s

"

It's pretty clear now that what looked like it might have been some kind of counterculture is, in reality, just the plain old chaos of undifferentiated weirdness.

"

Jerry Garcia
Founding member and lead guitarist of the Grateful Dead, and counterculture icon

---

"

If you're going to kick authority in the teeth, you might as well use two feet.

"

Keith Richards
Guitarist and founding member of the Rolling Stones

Summer of Love

The 1967 "Summer of Love" saw thousands of young people gathering in the Haight-Ashbury district of San Francisco to celebrate peace, love and music.

Characterized by hippie fashion and ideals, drug-taking and a spirit of communal living, it has become an iconic symbol of the 1960s counterculture movement.

"

If you're going to
San Francisco, be sure to wear
some flowers in your hair.

"

Scott McKenzie
From "San Francisco", 1967. The song sold
more than 7 million copies worldwide.

the nineteen

60s

Chapter **3**

in the groove

Pushing boundaries and embracing a sense of freedom and individuality, the music and style of the '60s reflected the rebellious spirit of the era. From The Beatles' catchy tunes to the brash sounds of The Who, music became a powerful medium of cultural expression.

In fashion, bold and iconic styles such as miniskirts, bell-bottoms and psychedelic prints broke all the rules.

Fashion Firsts

The 1960s was an era of experimentation and bold self-expression, leaving a lasting impact on fashion.

Women's clothes saw a revolution with miniskirts, go-go boots and psychedelic prints, while men's fashion experienced a shift towards more casual attire, influenced by The Beatles' iconic style.

"

In the 1960s, everyone
was doing their own thing.
We were all rebels.

"

Mary Quant
British fashion designer

Fab Four

At the start of 1963, The Beatles —
formed in Liverpool in 1960 — were a little-
known rock band. By the year's end, they
were riding a global wave of popularity
dubbed "Beatlemania". The ecstatic
fan culture saw screaming teenage girls
assembling wherever the band appeared.

"

This has gotten entirely out of control.

"

Saturday Evening Post, commenting on the rise of
"Beatlemania", March 1964

"

We were all on this ship
in the sixties, our generation,
a ship going to discover
the New World.
And The Beatles were in the
crow's nest of that ship.

"

John Lennon

"

I'd like to say thank you on behalf of the group and ourselves, and I hope we passed the audition.

"

John Lennon

Addressing the crowd during an impromptu concert performed on the rooftop of Apple Studios in London, 30 January 1969.
It was The Beatles' final public live performance.

Bad Boys of Rock

Formed in 1962, the Rolling Stones emerged as a rebellious force in the 1960s music scene. Led by Mick Jagger's charismatic stage presence and Keith Richards' iconic guitar riffs, the band's raw, blues-infused rock 'n' roll captivated audiences worldwide.

In 1967, a highly publicized drug bust at Richards' home further solidified the band's edgy reputation.

"

I'd rather be dead than sing 'Satisfaction' when I'm 45.

"

Mick Jagger

Blowin' in the Wind

Bob Dylan emerged as a key figure in the 1960s folk and protest music movement. His poetic lyrics and distinctive voice captured the spirit of the era, with songs such as "Blowin' in the Wind" becoming anthems for social change.

Dylan's introspective compositions established him as a voice of a generation, inspiring countless artists to use music as a means of expression.

"

Being noticed can be a
burden. Jesus got himself
crucified because he got himself
noticed. So I disappear a lot.

"

Bob Dylan

Twiggy

With her boyish frame, doe-like eyes and elfin haircut, British fashion model Twiggy became the face of the Swinging London era. Widely considered to be one of the world's first supermodels, she popularized an ultra-thin and youthful aesthetic.

As she gained international recognition, she appeared on magazine covers around the world, including leading fashion magazine *Vogue* in April 1967.

"

At 16, I was a funny, skinny
little thing, all eyelashes and legs.
And then, suddenly people told
me it was gorgeous. I thought
they had gone mad.

"

Twiggy
Reflecting on her career in modelling

Surfin' USA

Known for their sunny sounds and harmonious vocal arrangements, The Beach Boys captured the essence of California's surf culture, with hits like "Surfin' USA" and "Good Vibrations" becoming iconic anthems of the era. Led by Brian Wilson, the band's innovative production techniques and lush harmonies pushed the boundaries of popular music.

"

I made a dollar a day sweeping a laundry out. Then we made a record that was number two in Los Angeles. We got so excited hearing it on the radio that Carl threw up.

"

Dennis Wilson

Reflecting on The Beach Boys' rise to fame

Ten Big Bands

The Beatles

The iconic "Fab Four" came to personify the counterculture of the 1960s.

The Rolling Stones

Rock Royalty today, the Stones delivered timeless hits laced with rebellion.

The Beach Boys

The band's melodious sound came to define US surf culture.

The Doors

These rock pioneers hauntingly blended poetry and psychedelic rock.

The Jimi Hendrix Experience

Hendrix's guitar-playing virtuosity left an indelible mark on music.

Creedence Clearwater Revival
The American rock icons delivered swampy, bluesy hits.

The Kinks
The band blended iconic guitar riffs, social commentary and humour.

The Who
The rock legends' powerful anthems defined the Mod era.

Led Zeppelin
Combining blues and heavy riffs, the band set the standard for hard rock.

Pink Floyd
The progressive rock trailblazers created epic concept albums.

Jackie O Sunglasses

Jacqueline Kennedy, the First Lady of the US from 1961 to 1963, had a significant influence on fashion.

Known for her impeccable sense of style and elegance, she favoured tailored, clean-lined outfits, including sheath dresses, pillbox hats and chic suits.

Her oversized sunglasses became a signature accessory – known as "Jackie O" sunglasses, their popularity soared.

"

Pearls are always appropriate.

"

Jacqueline Kennedy

First Lady from 1961 until 1963

"

I see myself as a huge fiery comet, a shooting star. Everyone stops, points up and gasps 'Oh look at that!' Then – whoosh, and I'm gone... and they'll never see anything like it ever again... and they won't be able to forget me – ever.

"

Jim Morrison
Lead singer of The Doors

66

The '60s was one of the first times the power of music was used by a generation to bind them together.

99

Neil Young

66

It's an often-asked question, 'Why did all these spotty white English boys suddenly start playing blues in the '60s?' It was recognized as this kind of vibrant music and when I first started playing in a blues band, I just wanted to bring it to a wider public who hadn't really heard it.

99

Steve Winwood

"

Because Dickens and Dostoyevsky and Woody Guthrie were telling their stories much better than I ever could, I decided to stick to my own mind.

"

Bob Dylan
Sidney Fields interview, August 1963

Miniskirt

British designer Mary Quant is credited with pioneering the daring miniskirt. Challenging conventional hemlines, it symbolized the spirit of youthful rebellion and female empowerment.

Sparking controversy and fascination alike, it has become a powerful symbol of the cultural and social changes that defined the swinging '60s.

"

I didn't think of the mini as sexual but as an instrument of liberation. I wanted to make clothes that you could move in, skirts you could run and dance in, but, of course, wearing clothes like that made you feel and look sexy.

"

Mary Quant

Reflecting on her iconic creation, the miniskirt

Purple Haze

Iconic guitarist and songwriter Jimi Hendrix embodied the spirit of musical experimentation in the 1960s. With his innovative approach to guitar playing, he redefined the possibilities of the instrument.

Songs such as "Purple Haze" and "Hey Joe" showcased his unique blend of psychedelic rock, blues and soul, and solidified his status as a legendary figure in music history.

"

When the power of love overcomes the love of power, the world will know peace.

"

Jimi Hendrix

Hippie Fashion

Rebelling against a conformist society, hippies were focused on freedom and getting back to nature. Men and women grew their hair long, and anything handmade was prized. These five items were a key part of the hippie look:

Tie-dye clothing – this popular technique was used to create vibrant, psychedelic patterns.

Bell-bottom jeans – preferably adorned with a fringe at the ankle and flower patches, this style was seen everywhere.

Flower crowns – flower garlands and flower images painted on the face represented peace and love.

Patchwork clothing – patchwork designs showcased a DIY ethos and a celebration of individuality.

Peace symbol accessories – necklaces, earrings and pins showing this hippie symbol were all popular accessories.

Motown

This influential record label, founded in Detroit, Michigan, in 1959, had a profound impact on the music industry throughout the 1960s. With artists like The Supremes, Marvin Gaye and Stevie Wonder, Motown produced a string of chart-topping hits that crossed racial and cultural boundaries.

"

If you can't find peace within yourself, you'll never find it anywhere else.

"

Marvin Gaye

Psychedlic Rock

This vibrant genre emerged in the 1960s, blending elements of rock, folk and hallucinatory experiences.

Bands like The Beatles, The Doors and Jefferson Airplane made use of distorted guitar sounds, trippy lyrics and elaborate studio production techniques.

Five Psychedelic Rock Songs

"Strawberry Fields Forever"
The Beatles

"Space Oddity"
David Bowie

"A Whiter Shade of Pale"
Procol Harum

"Porpoise Song"
The Monkees

"Good Vibrations"
The Beach Boys

the nineteen

60s

Chapter **4**

winds of change

The 1960s witnessed a wave of protests that challenged the status quo and inspired future generations. Around the world, civil rights movements fought against racial discrimination, anti-war protests challenged the Vietnam War, student movements called for free speech and women's rights organizations demanded gender equality. In the words of Sam Cooke's iconic protest song, "A Change is Gonna Come".

I Have a Dream

Martin Luther King Jr's iconic speech, delivered during the 1963 March on Washington for Jobs and Freedom, is one of the most iconic speeches in American history.

Urging the nation to rise above hatred and injustice and to embrace the ideals of freedom, justice and equality for all, he passionately called for racial equality and an end to segregation in America.

66

I have a dream that my four little children will one day live in a nation where they will not be judged by the colour of their skin but by the content of their character...

99

Martin Luther King Jr
Speech delivered from the steps of the Lincoln Memorial, March on Washington, 28 August 1963

"

The time is always right to do what is right.

"

Martin Luther King Jr
Speech in Birmingham, Alabama, 12 April 1963

"

I would say that I'm a
nonviolent soldier. In place of
weapons of violence, you have to
use your mind, your heart, your
sense of humour, every faculty
available to you.

"

Joan Baez
American folk singer and activist

Death of an Icon

Tragically, Martin Luther King Jr was assassinated on 4 April 1968, in Memphis, Tennessee. As he stood on the balcony of the Lorraine Motel, he was shot by James Earl Ray.

His death – which sparked widespread outrage and grief, and sent shockwaves throughout the world – was a devastating blow to the civil rights movement that he had tirelessly championed.

66

A man dies when he refuses to stand up for that which is right. A man dies when he refuses to stand up for justice. A man dies when he refuses to take a stand for that which is true.

99

Martin Luther King Jr

From a sermon given at Selma, Alabama, on 8 March 1965, the day after "Bloody Sunday", on which civil rights protesters were attacked and beaten by police on the Edmund Pettus Bridge

"

Let us close the springs of racial poison. Let us pray for wise and understanding hearts. Let us lay aside irrelevant differences and make our nation whole.

"

Lyndon B. Johnson
Remarks on signing the Civil Rights Act, 2 July 1964

66

You can't separate peace from freedom because no one can be at peace unless he has his freedom.

99

Malcolm X
Influential member of the Black Power movement, speech in New York, 7 January 1965

We Shall Overcome

This powerful gospel song became closely associated with the civil rights movement. In 1963, folksinger Joan Baez led a 300,000-strong crowd in singing the anthem during the March on Washington.

Five years later, in March 1968, Martin Luther King, Jr recited words from the song in his final sermon, just days before his death. It would be sung at his funeral a few days later.

"

Oh, deep in my heart
I know that I do believe
We shall overcome, someday.

We shall live in peace
We shall live in peace
We shall live in peace, someday.

"

From the gospel song "We Shall Overcome",
which became closely associated with the
civil rights movement

Women's Rights

The women's liberation movement emerged as a powerful force in the 1960s. Inspired by civil rights and anti-war movements, women began challenging traditional gender roles, and demanding equal pay and an end to discrimination.

The formation of organizations such as NOW (National Organization for Women) in the US, and the Women's Liberation Movement (WLM) in the UK, sparked a wave of activism.

"

If society stopped telling girls that men can and should hand them their total identity on a silver platter, wives wouldn't be so resentful when it didn't happen.

"

Gloria Steinem
New York magazine, 23 December 1968

"

At least through most of
the 1960s, I basically lived
in a man's world, hardly
speaking to a woman all day
except to the secretaries.

"

Katharine Graham

American businesswoman who led
The Washington Post from 1963 until 1991

"

The only way to support a revolution is to make your own.

"

Abbie Hoffman

American social and political activist

The Feminine Mystique

The publication of Betty Friedan's groundbreaking book was a pivotal moment in the women's liberation movement. The *The Feminine Mystique* challenged the prevailing view that women's fulfillment solely rested on being wives and mothers.

Resonating with countless women, it encouraged them to question societal expectations and seek better opportunities.

66

The problem that has no name — which is simply the fact that American women are kept from growing to their full human capacities — is taking a far greater toll on the physical and mental health of our country than any known disease.

99

Betty Friedan
The Feminine Mystique, 1963

"

A woman needs a man like a fish needs a bicycle.

"

Irina Dunn

1960s feminist slogan

"

We can change ourselves with
feminine intelligence and awareness,
into a basically organic, non-competitive
society that is based on love, rather than
reasoning. The result will be a society of
balance, peace and contentment.
We can evolve rather than revolt, come
together rather than claim independence,
and feel rather than think.

"

Yoko Ono

Emerging onto the international art scene in the
early 1960s, Yoko Ono pioneered the idea of feminism
in artistic practice

May '68

The French student protests of May 1968 were sparked by discontent over the conservative policies of President Charles de Gaulle. Starting in Paris, the unrest quickly spread across France, encompassing workers' strikes and broader societal demands for change – and came close to bringing down the French government.

Ultimately suppressed, the protests left a lasting impact – and are still an iconic symbol of countercultural power.

"
Soyez réalistes, demandez l'impossible!
„

French slogan, meaning "Be realistic, demand the impossible!", from the student protests of May '68

Anti-Vietnam War Movement

The 1960s witnessed a powerful surge of anti-war protests, fuelled by opposition to the Vietnam War and a desire for peace. Activists, students and citizens took to the streets, rallying against the conflict and demanding an end to the violence.

These protests showcased a generation's growing disillusionment with government policies, sparked debates on national priorities and shaped public opinion.

" Make love, not war. "

These iconic words became a rallying cry during the 1960s anti-war protests

" The whole world is watching. "

Phrase chanted by anti-Vietnam War demonstrators as
they were beaten and arrested by police outside
the Conrad Hilton Hotel in Chicago, 1968

"

You're old enough to kill,
but not for votin'

You don't believe in war, but
what's that gun you're totin'?

"

Barry McGuire
"Eve of Destruction", 1965

" Wanted: President Johnson for crimes against humanity. "

Slogan from an anti-Vietnam-War march,
Sydney, Australia, 1 February 1966

"NO"

The single word on a poster designed by Ian Maclaren,
accompanied by a mushroom cloud image, for CND
(Campaign for Nuclear Disarmament), 1967

Stonewall Riots

In June 1969, a series of spontaneous demonstrations by the LGBTQ+ community took place in New York City. The riots broke out at the Stonewall Inn, a gay bar in Greenwich Village. These protests marked a significant turning point in the fight for LGBTQ+ rights, sparking a new era of activism.

The riots served as a catalyst for the formation of LGBTQ+ organizations and the broader struggle for equality and liberation.

"
I'm not missing a moment of this – it's the revolution!
"

Sylvia Rivera
Latin-American drag queen, at the
Stonewall Riots, 28 June 1969

"

It is not our differences that divide us. It is our inability to recognize, accept and celebrate those differences.

"

Audre Lorde
1960s activist who described herself as
"black, lesbian, feminist, mother, poet, warrior"

"

Injustice anywhere is a threat to justice everywhere.

"

Martin Luther King Jr
"Letter from a Birmingham Jail", addressing
his fellow clergymen, 16 April 1963

the nineteen 60s

Chapter 5

man on the moon

In July 1969, the world watched mesmerized as the astronauts of *Apollo 11* became the first humans to walk on the moon. It was the close of a decade that had seen computers becoming more accessible, key breakthroughs in telecommunications and the birth of the Internet.

The launch of the contraceptive pill became a gamechanger for women's lives, while the world's first successful heart transplant was a medical milestone.

The Space Race

In a major milestone for space exploration, Soviet Cosmonaut Yuri Gagarin made history on 12 April 1961, becoming the first person to journey into space. He completed one orbit around the Earth.

Just one month later, American astronaut Alan Shepard followed suit, becoming the first American to venture into space with a suborbital flight aboard the Freedom 7 spacecraft.

66

We choose to go to the Moon in this decade and do the other things, not because they are easy, but because they are hard; because that goal will serve to organize and measure the best of our energies and skills, because that challenge is one that we are willing to accept, one we are unwilling to postpone, and one we intend to win, and the others, too.

99

John F. Kennedy
Speech to bolster support for his proposal to land
a man on the moon before 1970, 12 September 1962

Spacewar!

This instantly addictive video game was developed in 1962 by Steve Russell. One of the earliest digital computer games, it simulated space combat between two spaceships. Players used control inputs to manoeuvre and fire at each other, navigating the gravitational pull of a star at the centre of the screen.

Spacewar! remained the most popular video game on most computer systems for more than a decade.

❝

If I hadn't done it, someone would've done something equally exciting, if not better, in the next six months. I just happened to get there first.

❞

Steve Russell

Reflecting on his pioneering video game, Spacewar!

The Pill

The launch of the birth control pill in 1960 was a milestone in women's liberation.

Although it would be several years before it was widely available, the pill provided a reliable method of contraception and empowered women to plan their families, pursue education and careers, and enjoy more autonomy in their personal lives.

"

Young women don't realize what
hell it was [before the arrival of
the pill]... The perpetual anxiety.
It was a real revolution.

"

Mary Quant
The iconic fashion designer reflects on how
the pill transformed women's lives

Eight Advertising Slogans

"It's the real thing"

Coca-Cola

"Think small"

Volkswagen

"A Mars a day helps you work, rest and play"

Mars Bar

"We fix Sunday dinner seven nights a week"

KFC

"For sheer driving pleasure"
BMW

**"Plop, plop, fizz, fizz,
oh what a relief it is"**
Alka Seltzer

"Buckle down with Nixon"
Nixon presidential campaign

"Put a tiger in your tank"
Esso

Four Incredible Inventions

Compact Cassette – invented by Philips in 1962

Computer Mouse – developed by Douglas Engelbart in 1964

Laser Technology – Theodore Maiman demonstrated the first working laser in 1960

Hypertext – first introduced by Ted Nelson in the 1960s

66

A man may die, nations may rise and fall but an idea lives on.

99

John F. Kennedy

Remarks recorded at the opening of a USIA transmitter at Greenville, North Carolina, 8 February 1963

Silent Spring

In 1962, influential environmentalist and author Rachel Carson helped set the stage for the modern environmental movement with her book *Silent Spring*.

Her research and writing on the dangers of pesticides and pollution helped raise awareness about the importance of environmental conservation and questioned humanity's faith in technological progress.

"

We stand now where two roads diverge. But unlike the roads in Robert Frost's familiar poem, they are not equally fair. The road we have long been travelling is deceptively easy, a smooth superhighway on which we progress with great speed, but at its end lies disaster. The other fork of the road – the one less travelled by – offers our last, our only chance to reach a destination that assures the preservation of the earth.

"

Rachel Carson
Silent Spring, 1962

Lunar Landing

On 20 July 1969, NASA's *Apollo 11* mission successfully landed astronauts Neil Armstrong and Buzz Aldrin on the moon's surface. Around the world, an estimated 650 million viewers gathered around television sets to share this historic moment.

Marking a new era of human exploration and achievement, it remains one of the most watched events in television history.

"

One small step for man, one giant leap for mankind.

"

Neil Armstrong

The astronaut's words as he first stepped onto the moon,
20 July 1969

Computer Revolution

The 1960s marked a period of rapid development in computer technology. The concept of time-sharing emerged, enabling multiple users to access a computer simultaneously.

In 1964, IBM introduced the IBM System/360 mainframe computers, which allowed organizations to process large volumes of data and run complex applications.

" But what... is it good for? "

Engineer at the Advanced Computing Systems Division
of IBM, commenting on the microchip, 1968

Pioneering Transplant

On 3 December 1967, the first successful heart transplant was performed by South African surgeon Dr Christiaan Barnard, in Cape Town. The recipient was a 53-year-old man suffering from heart failure and the donor was a 25-year-old woman who had died in a car accident.

Although the man died 18 days after the transplant due to pneumonia, this pioneering surgery paved the way for further advancements in organ transplantation.

“

On Saturday, I was a surgeon
in South Africa, very little
known. On Monday, I was
world-renowned.

”

Christiaan Barnard
Surgeon who carried out the first human heart transplant

These five innovations have barely changed since they were first launched in the 1960s:

Bubble Wrap – invented in 1960 by engineers Alfred Fielding and Marc Chavannes as a textured wallpaper, it soon found popularity as protective packaging material.

Aspartame – the artificial sweetener was discovered in 1965 by chemist James Schlatter while working on an anti-ulcer drug.

Sharpie – The beloved permanent marker was invented in 1964 by Sidney Rosenthal.

Correction Fluid – Invented by Bette Nesmith Graham in the early 1960s, she created the fluid to conveniently correct typing errors.

Lava Lamp – Edward Craven Walker invented the "Astro Lamp" in 1963. The unique combination of wax and coloured liquid created mesmerizing patterns when heated.

Staying Connected

The first communication satellite, Telestar, was launched in 1962, enabling live television broadcasts and long-distance telephone calls across the Atlantic Ocean. In 1963, the development of the touch-tone telephone revolutionized phone dialling and paved the way for automated customer service systems.

Internet Milestone

In an historic moment, the precursor to the Internet, ARPANET, facilitated its first data transmission between the University of California, Los Angeles (UCLA) and Stanford University, in 1969.

The successful relay of communications laid the foundation for the transformative power of the Internet, shaping global connectivity as we know it today.

the nineteen

60s

Chapter 6
popular culture

The 1960s saw a burst of creative talent. Groundbreaking films such as *The Graduate* and *Psycho* wowed audiences and critics alike while Pop Art and Op Art revolutionized the visual arts. Harper Lee's coming-of-age novel, *To Kill a Mockingbird*, captured the hearts of millions of readers around the world, and boxing legend Muhammad Ali became one of the decade's most iconic figures.

To Kill a Mockingbird

Harper Lee's groundbreaking novel, published in 1960, swiftly became a literary phenomenon. Set in the 1930s, in America's Deep South, the book tackles themes of racial injustice, innocence and the loss of childhood. Through the eyes of Scout Finch, the story explores her father's defence of a black man accused of rape and the moral conflicts that arise.

The book's enduring relevance and powerful storytelling have made it a classic of American literature.

"

Mockingbirds don't do one thing but make music for us to enjoy. They don't eat up people's gardens, don't nest in corncribs, they don't do one thing but sing their hearts out for us. That's why it's a sin to kill a mockingbird.

"

Harper Lee
To Kill a Mockingbird, 1960

Sixties Slang

Groovy – stylish or cool

Far Out – expressing amazement

Cool – groovy, or calm and collected

Dig It – to be into something

Peace – a hippie greeting

Dude – a person, usually a man

Mellow – relaxed and laid back

Psychedelic – associated with mind-altering experiences

Square – very uncool

Mod – short for "modern", representing the youth fashion movement

Hollywood Legend

In August 1962, iconic American actress Marilyn Monroe passed away at the age of 36. Her death was ruled as a probable suicide by drug overdose.

Known for her mesmerizing beauty, captivating performances and tumultuous personal life, her death sparked countless conspiracy theories and heightened her status as a timeless Hollywood legend.

66

Imperfection is beauty,
madness is genius and it's better
to be absolutely ridiculous than
absolutely boring.

99

Marilyn Monroe

Bond: "I admire your courage Miss...?"

Silvia: "Trench. Silvia Trench. I admire your luck Mr...?"

Bond: "Bond. James Bond."

Sean Connery
The actor utters James Bond's iconic phrase for the first time in the film *Dr No*, 1962

"

Mrs Robinson, you're trying to seduce me.

"

Dustin Hoffman

In the role of Benjamin Braddock, *The Graduate*, 1967

Five Fabulous Films

2001: A Space Odyssey
dir. Stanley Kubrick (1968)

This visionary science fiction film pushed the boundaries of filmmaking with its stunning visuals and philosophical exploration of human evolution.

Psycho
dir. Alfred Hitchcock (1960)

Considered a masterpiece of suspense, this psychological drama wowed and shocked audiences with its innovative storytelling and infamous shower scene.

The Graduate,
dir. Mike Nichols (1967)

With its memorable soundtrack, the romantic comedy captured the disillusionment and alienation of the younger generation.

Breathless,
dir. Jean-Luc Godard (1960)

The unconventional style and narrative techniques of this French New Wave film revolutionized cinema.

Bonnie and Clyde
dir. Arthur Penn (1967)

Blending violence and dark humour, *Bonnie and Clyde* challenged traditional Hollywood storytelling.

Birth of a Legend

On 25 February 1964, boxer Muhammad Ali – then known as Cassius Clay – shocked the world by defeating the heavily favoured Sonny Liston to claim the heavyweight title.

The victory catapulted Ali into boxing superstardom and set the stage for his remarkable journey as one of the greatest boxers of all time.

" Float like a butterfly, sting like a bee. "

Muhammad Ali

"

Some people are on the pitch! They think it's all over! It is now!

"

Kenneth Wolstenholme

The iconic quote made while commentating on the 1966 FIFA World Cup final between England and West Germany. With England leading 3-2 in extra time, Geoff Hurst scored his third goal, sealing England's victory.

"

In 1968, in the midst of the tumultuous 1960s, the Olympics were much more than just another event.

"

Peggy Fleming
Figure skater and winner of the United States' only Olympic gold at the 1968 Winter Games

---

❝

Although it is hard to believe,
the sixties are not fictional;
they actually happened.

❞

Stephen King
Hearts in Atlantis, 1999

"

Sexual intercourse began
In nineteen sixty-three
(Which was rather late for me)
Between the end of the
Chatterley ban
And The Beatles' first LP.

"

Philip Larkin
"Annus Mirabilis", 1967

Groundbreaking Novels

Catch-22
Joseph Heller (1961)

Following the experiences of American bomber pilots during the Second World War, this satirical novel critiques the illogicality of war.

The Golden Notebook
Doris Lessing, 1962

Lessing's daring novel, about a mother and novelist suffering a mental breakdown, was hailed by women at the time as the "feminist Bible".

A Single Man
Christopher Isherwood, 1965

Exploring a day in the life of a gay English professor, this pioneering work about a man struggling to come to terms with his sexuality was way ahead of its time.

In Cold Blood
Truman Capote (1966)

Based on a true story, but written as a novel, Capote's innovative work presents a chilling account of the brutal murder of the Clutter family in rural Kansas, in America's Midwest.

One Hundred Years of Solitude
Gabriel García Márquez (1967)

This landmark work of magical realism tells the story of the Buendía family across multiple generations, exploring themes of love, time and the cyclical nature of history.

66

Fear, after all, is our real enemy.
Fear is taking over our world...
Think about it. Fear that we're going
to be attacked, fear that there are
communists lurking around every corner,
fear that some little Caribbean country
that doesn't believe in our way of life
poses a threat to us. Fear that black
culture may take over the world. Fear
of Elvis Presley's hips...

99

Christopher Isherwood
A Single Man, 1965

" Welcome to the post-pill paradise... "

John Updike

Couples, 1968. This novel, following the sex lives of
ten American couples, catapulted its author onto
the cover of *Time* magazine.

The trombones crunched redgold under my bed, and behind my gulliver the trumpets three-wise silverflamed, and there by the door the timps rolling through my guts and out again crunched like candy thunder. Oh, it was wonder of wonders.

Anthony Burgess
Describing Beethoven, *A Clockwork Orange*, 1962.
This groundbreaking novel is set in a future society overrun by youth violence.

"

Fertile in invention, rich in humour, acutely observant, he depicts fantastic characters who are recognizable as exaggerations of real types, and situations only slightly more absurd than those that happen daily, and he lets his imagination rip in fairyland.

"

From a review of Roald Dahl's *Charlie and the Chocolate Factory*, *The New York Times*, 25 October 1964

Top Toys

From dolls and action figures to model kits and outdoor playsets, the 1960s brought toys that entertained, educated and inspired generations of children.

Etch A Sketch – Introduced in 1960, the Etch A Sketch drawing toy allowed users to create images by controlling a stylus that drew on a grey screen.

GI Joe – Launched in 1964, this popular action figure, marketed to boys, became a cultural icon.

Easy-Bake Oven – This beloved toy, launched in 1963 by Hasbro, became a must-have item for aspiring young chefs.

Barbie – The iconic doll was first introduced by Mattel in 1959 but remained immensely popular throughout the 1960s.

Hot Wheels – Launched by Mattel in 1968, these miniature die-cast vehicles sparked a collecting craze.

Sea-Monkeys

These instant pets became one of the most popular toys of all time in the 1960s.

The "creatures from the sea" – in reality, brine shrimp – were sold in kits that allowed owners to hatch and observe them in a small aquarium.

Sales rocketed and Sea Monkeys ads graced the back pages of comic books everywhere.

" Own a bowlful of happiness – Instant Pets! "

From an advert for Sea Monkeys,
which were introduced in 1960

Pop Art

Challenging traditional notions of high art, this movement celebrated popular culture, consumerism and celebrity. Incorporating imagery from mass media, advertising and everyday objects, artists such as Andy Warhol and Roy Lichtenstein reproduced familiar images through techniques such as screen printing and comic-book-style dots.

"
Pop art is for everyone.
"

Andy Warhol
Leading figure in the Pop Art movement

"

Pop Art looks out into the world. It doesn't look like a painting of something, it looks like the thing itself.

"

Roy Lichtenstein
Leading figure in the Pop Art movement

"

In the future, everyone will be world-famous for 15 minutes.

"

Andy Warhol

From a brochure distributed at one of his exhibitions, 1968

Five Art Movements

Minimalism sought to strip art down to its essential elements, focusing on simplicity, geometry and industrial materials.

Fluxus was an interdisciplinary movement that blurred the boundaries between art and life, emphasizing collective creativity and audience participation.

Op Art, short for "optical art", used optical illusions, geometric patterns and vibrant colours to create visually striking effects.

Conceptual Art placed emphasis on the idea or concept behind the artwork, rather than its physical form.

Feminist Art emerged in the 1960s as a response to the social and political inequalities faced by women, and aimed to challenge patriarchal norms and highlight women's experiences and perspectives.

"

Well, I'm not interested in the kind of expression you have when you paint a painting with brushstrokes. It's all right, but its already done and I want to do something new.

"

Donald Judd
Prominent minimalist artist from the 1960s

66

There was a time when meanings were focused and reality could be fixed; when that sort of belief disappeared, things became uncertain and open to interpretation.

99

Bridget Riley

Prominent figure in the Op Art movement

"

If you can remember anything about the sixties, you weren't really there.

"

Paul Kantner

Co-founder of leading psychedelic
rock band Jefferson Airplane